7 STEPS TO MASTER YOUR HEART & MIND

A Step-by-Step Guide to Reclaim the Power of Controlling How You Feel and What You Think

JOSHUA HENRY

7 STEPS TO MASTER YOUR HEART & MIND

A Step-by-Step Guide to Reclaim the Power of Controlling How You Feel and What You Think

Printed in the United States of America

DEDICATION

I dedicate this page to my mother, brother, and everyone who has taken it upon themselves to break generational curses. I also want to dedicate this page to everyone who seeks to learn more about themselves. Essentially, I hope this book brings insight into how you can master and love yourself completely, thus authorizing you to live out your biggest aspirations. Believing in yourself is the key to this book and your journey.

EXECUTION STATEMENT

Take a moment to write this execution statement on a separate piece of paper. Share it on Instagram and tag me @injoshua_wetrust_. Share your goal of consistently practicing with someone who can help hold you accountable. Your ability to master your heart and mind is equal to the effort you put into these practices regularly. Even the most gifted individuals are nothing without consistency, effort, and determination.

I am committed to seeing this process through from start to finish so I can reclaim control of what I think and how I feel, which will allow me to live my best life.

I am willing to love every aspect of myself no matter how long it takes me.

Sign ______________________________

Date ______________________________

Write three names or reasons why you are doing this. If you ever think about quitting, you can look back and gather the willpower not to let them or yourself down.

1.

2.

3..

CONTENTS

Dedication i
Execution Statement iii
About the Author 1

Introduction: The Three A's 3
STEP 1: Remembering Who You Are 7
STEP 2: Being In the Here-and-Now 15
STEP 3: What You Think, You Become 21
STEP 4: Emotionally Accept Whatever is Here-and-Now 27
STEP 5: Trust 33
STEP 6: Breathing 41
STEP 7: Love Unconditionally 47

Resources 59

ABOUT THE AUTHOR

I am an aspiring award-winning author, life coach, philosopher, and humanitarian, born in New York but raised in Connecticut. My accomplishments to date exemplify the fortitude to endure life's hardships in order to courageously follow my heart. From having to flee from New York as an infant from an abusive father who attempted to kill my mother and me, through relocating from relative to relative, to my mother later marrying another man who was also abusive and spoke negatively throughout that time, life has taught me many strenuous lessons. I've had the pleasure to endure the experiences of loved ones passing, never having a father figure or a positive male role model, coping with physical ailments, and falling prey to the world.

Nonetheless, at the age of 19, I slowly began to question everything under the umbrella of life, including my life's purpose. I gradually started reading, meditating, praying, and practicing the knowledge that would transform my life. It has all led me to this point, where I have remembered my soul's mission. Life has led me to this opportunity to utilize my depth and gifts to creatively help others love themselves completely and demonstrate how they too can transmute their darkness into their greatest blessings.

My mission is to help others transform their darkness into their power to illuminate their lives and reawaken their conscious awareness. In doing so, more and more people will learn to love themselves and project that same love onto others around them. This is one of many books that I will be creating with the hope of bringing humanity back to love. I've created this book to be used as a guide for all human beings to learn about and master themselves so that they can live out their unique dreams. I have also created a 1-on-1 coaching program for anyone who is determined to learn more about themselves to ultimately master themselves. Through my mother's protective actions, I have been kept alive to see this day. I am blessed to be able to share this knowledge with you all.

INTRODUCTION
THE THREE A'S

Welcome to the 7 steps to master your heart and mind. In this book, you will relearn who you are, how to control how you feel minute-by-minute, and how to effectively use your mind. In order to have this written, I had to face all my emotions, demons, fears, insecurities, flaws, and expectations I imposed onto others (including myself). By doing so, I took full responsibility for my life and freed myself from the imprisonment of my mind. As a result, I have transformed my darkness into my strength and ally, and I wish to establish how you can, too. It is now your turn to transmute your darkness into your power and consciously co-create the life you desire!

I will teach and use the following seven steps as exercises that will enable you to unlock the suppressed parts of yourself to then accept and love yourself just as you are, here and now.

- Step 1 - Remembering Who You Are
- Step 2 - Being In the Here-and-Now
- Step 3 - What You Think, You Become
- Step 4 - Emotionally Accept Whatever is Here-and-Now
- Step 5 - Trust
- Step 6 - Breathing
- Step 7 - Love Unconditionally

Before the first step, it is necessary to lay out three fundamental understandings that will help prepare you to undergo your awakening journey. Allow me to say this process will not be easy and requires dedication. You must be willingly prepared to go within yourself to confront all your traumatic experiences. In exchange for confronting and accepting them, you will be gifted with control of your heart and mind.

The three fundamental understandings are:

- Accountability
- Acceptance
- Awareness

Let's quickly break these down, starting with accountability. Understand that whatever you think, say, or do, you become. No one else is responsible for your words or actions. Deflection and avoidance will keep you trapped in the illusion that it's the fault of the world for making you act out. This perceived illusion will keep you tense and make you feel as though you have no control over yourself. To break free, you have to stand up for yourself and own up to your actions, thoughts, and decisions (no matter how "good" or "bad" they are). This is your life, your body, your mind, and your heart; no one else can assume responsibility for it.

The next fundamental understanding is acceptance. Living life with a degree of acceptance allows you to live harmoniously within yourself and with other people. It is the key to calming your rational mind of worry, anxiety, anger, fear, etc. We will touch upon it in greater detail in Chapter Four.

The third understanding, and the most important of the three, is awareness. It is the space where you can peacefully perceive what you feel and think without attaching yourself to those emotions and thoughts. Awareness will be what allows you to practice controlling your heart and mind. Through awareness, you will learn how to shift your thoughts from unpleasant to uplifting. This may sound difficult at first, but with practice, you will learn how to with ease.

These three fundamental understandings are created to serve as a model to prepare you to begin shifting your attention inwardly. Now, before we dive into the seven steps, it is crucial to your journey that you continuously practice the three understandings alongside the seven steps. With consistent practice, you will truly reap the benefits of this book. As with any hobby or craft, through practice comes mastery. Be patient with yourself; do not compare your growth to that of anyone else's, and strive to love yourself unconditionally. This isn't a race or a contest. This is your heart and mind we are talking about. Let us treat this with delicacy, warmth, and persistence.

Let's begin!

STEP 1
REMEMBERING WHO YOU ARE

In this chapter, I will question and challenge your current belief system on who you perceive yourself to be. To begin, you must understand and know your origin. We all are created by the same creator that has no beginning or end. Our creator has multiple names among many languages and religious beliefs: God, Source, Love, the Universe, Allah, Jehovah, Abba, Elohim, or YAHWEH. Regardless of the title, we all are referring to the same creator. The creator of galaxies, stars, and planets is also the same creator who created us. By being created from this infinite intelligence, we are creators by default, inheriting the power to co-create the lives we desire. Your heart, mind, and body are the powerful resources given to you to have your dreams realized in this life. But notice how I referred to your heart, mind, and body as resources, meaning they do not define you. Your true essence is sheer conscious awareness. You are the awareness that oversees the screenplay of life. Your body and mind are partaking in the daily screenplay of interacting, planning, functioning, playing, feeling, and doing. But, it is not YOU who is doing these things (Keyes, 1975). You have always been the observer, and once you come to recognize this truth, you will then commence learning how to master your heart and mind. These are all things you already knew, but due to two things, you've been made hyper-reactive because you have been conditioned to be less aware of who you are and your innate power to create.

The two blockages are your emotional programming and your ego. Your emotional programming is the assortment of your wants, expectations, needs, and demands for which your ego directs most of your awareness and vitality on, both consciously and unconsciously (Keyes, 1975). This programming has been built into your consciousness throughout your years as a child. Through experiencing being sorely dominated, ruled over, and forcefully instructed on what to do and feel when you were an infant, you cultivated your emotional program. Your emotional programming consists of sensation, dominion, and stability fixations (any longing that makes you troubled or unhappy if it's not fulfilled) (Keyes, 1975). An example of a sensation fixation is the compulsiveness of wanting sex. An example of a dominion fixation is the need to control anything outside of yourself. An example of a stability fixation is the fear of losing money.

When any of these fixations are not satisfied, it is usually due to the outside world not conforming to the programmed pattern in your mind; this generates an uncomfortable emotional response and inserts you in a state of fight-or-flight. Despite getting older as years go by, your emotional programming remains the same until you consciously reprogram it. To do this, you will need to be conscious of the emotional programming you play out in your moment-to-moment experiences. The best way to become aware of your programming is to interact with people who irritate or provoke you emotionally. If you notice that you become frustrated when you are with a certain person, acknowledge this fact and ask yourself what about them makes you feel frustrated. It is important that you consciously tune into your emotions in your moment-to-moment experience. With this awareness, you will begin to notice when your ego triggers an emotional response you've been programmed to experience. Once you become aware, you then have the opportunity to choose a different response that promotes a more loving attitude. Permit life and those around you to assist in uncovering your emotional programming around your sensation, dominion, and stability fixations so that you can reprogram them to live a happier and more fulfilling life.

The other blockage that keeps many of us less aware of who we truly are as the conscious awareness is the ego. The ego is the mind-made image of itself, which can be seen as the leading force that controls your mind and emotions. It stops you from perceiving reality as it is. Instead, through the lens of the ego, you perceive others as objects from which you can obtain something (sex, food, money) or as a threat to your stature (Keyes, 1975). This keeps you tense and stuck in your emotional programming. You tend to stop seeing other people as human beings and more as tools and stepping stones to be manipulated in order to attain more sensation, dominion, and stability. This permits your rational mind to judge, scrutinize, and strategize others in a manner that will find ways to fulfill your fixations (Keyes, 1975). When your fixations are not satisfied, your ego triggers unpleasant emotions such as disappointment, fear, anger, worry, and frustration. Therefore, when you allow your ego to run your life, you will be emotionally triggered whenever the outside world does not yield how you want it to. Your ego will then reinforce your rational mind to continue to overthink and over-identify with the triggered emotion.

To begin tackling your ego, you must be aware of your perception of yourself. A great way to tell "what you think you are" or "who you think you are" is to carefully discern what your ego is shielding (Keyes, 1975). To indicate this, recognize how you feel when someone says something negative about your belief in who you are. If you become uptight and defensive, that is what your ego is desperately preserving. Have you ever noticed how most of us answer with our current social role, occupation, passion, and/or hobby when asked, "Who are you?" For example, "I am a mother of two," "I am a professional chef," and "I am an artist." We have been programmed to over-identify with our jobs and social roles. Some of us have been programmed to identify with what our loved ones numerously titled us as. Both of these are false depictions of who you truly are. You ARE NOT your experiences, your mind, your body, your job, your hobbies, your thoughts, your emotions, or what other people label you as. You are the conscious soul that oversees the human experience of the here and now. You have arrived at a point in life where you can choose to stop observing life through the lens of the ego (insecurity) and start observing from your authentic, higher self. This higher perspective frees you of pressing requests and expectations which your mind imposes on you. Reclaim your power as the conscious awareness that is the "spectator" watching your mind and body interact with other minds and bodies in this game we call life (Keyes, 1975).

At the end of each step, there will be exercises I encourage you to practice. Keep in mind that knowledge is of no value if it is not put into practice. This step will be one of the hardest because for many years you have been associated with and dominated by your ego. It will take time to disassociate with your ego and reconnect with your conscious awareness (higher self).

PRACTICES FOR CHAPTER 1

EXERCISE 1A.

When interacting with others, become aware of how you feel minute-by-minute. Whenever a triggering emotion surfaces, ask yourself two things: "What specific emotion am I experiencing?" and "What do I want to change in the world instead of doing the inner work of changing my response to it?"

EXERCISE 1B.

After pinpointing the root and cause of your triggering emotion, begin to reprogram your emotional pattern by rephrasing your thoughts. For example, instead of "I hate it when people cut me off while driving," rephrase it to, "I am learning how to peacefully control my emotions while driving."

EXERCISE 2.

Make a list of all the features, activities, and personal characteristics your ego safeguards. Make a copy for yourself. Burn one of them as a visual representation of freeing yourself from tirelessly defending your ego. Affirm (when needed) with "I am not my mind. I am not my body. I am not my thoughts or feelings. I am allowing myself to be free from all demands and expectations I impose on myself."

HE OR SHE WHO DEFINES THEMSELVES, CANNOT KNOW WHO THEY REALLY ARE

– LAO TZU

STEP 2

BEING IN THE HERE-AND-NOW

Welcome to step two! In this chapter, I want to talk to you about living in the present moment, here and now. The truth of reality is that there is no such thing as "time." Indeed, time is nothing more than an illusion created by humans. It was initially conceptualized by the Egyptians and Babylonians. They introduced calendars to organize and coordinate public events and to regulate cycles of planting and harvesting. Fast forward to today; we as human beings have evolved exponentially. Consequently, our lives heavily revolve around the construct of time, to the degree that we have created the concept of "past," "present," and "future." These are mind-made, nothing more than a fallacy. What has always been and will always be, is now. It is in the nowness of life that we are able to create. The past is extinct, and the future can only be envisioned. Yet, so many of us get caught indulging in them within our minds here and now. Being in your moment-to-moment experience, once the observer becomes aware of itself, you can then choose thoughts that will provoke cheerful emotions, leading to inspired action on what you wish to create in that very moment; this is what many refer to as manifesting. The innate ability to co-create your life experience is truly powerful when you deliberately live in the now. Chapter One is built as a catalyst to help you attune with your conscious awareness so that you can intentionally live in the now.

When you live in accordance with your ego and do not perceive who you truly are, your mind creates invisible prison bars that withhold you from being present. The control of the ego is immense in that it can influence your mind to fixate and be consumed by your traumatic life experiences and/or "what if's." Both thoughts evoke the emotion of sadness, depression, restlessness, uncertainty, and discontentment. We tend to suffer more in our thoughts than in reality, missing the opportunity to simply just be in the now. When you start living in the now, you step away from the observation of your mind, and your stream of thought begins to slow down, leading you to focus more of your attention on what is here and now (Tolle, 2003). For example, a couple has a heated argument and they mutually decide to break up. Fast forward a month later; one of them is consumed by their emotional programming and ego so much so that the entire month, all they have been able to do is analyze the situation and compute why things didn't work out. However, the other partner understands that they are not their thoughts or feelings. This enabled them to feel their emotions, release them, and continue living in the now. As a result, they started the business they always aspired to begin. The moral of the story is that we see things not as they are, but as we are (Keyes, 1975).

If you are not enjoying every second of your life, it is due to your wants, attachments, expectations, and demands on how life should "behave" towards you. All of these reinforce your emotional programming fixations, and because of that, we tend to dwell more in the deceased past or the envisioned future. Your experience of this moment and every moment moving forward is conceived by the program in your mind (Keyes, 1975). Whenever you are consumed by overwhelming thoughts, you are evading the now. Ultimately, you cannot take control of your life unless you take responsibility for this moment, here and now (Tolle, 2003). Since all we have is now, I challenge you to embrace it. Become cordial with it and focus your attention upon your moment-to-moment experience. Watch how your inner peace develops as your stream of thoughts dwindles.

PRACTICES FOR CHAPTER 2

EXERCISE 1.

In any alone time or when you're idle, turn your attention to the thoughts passing through your mind, any bodily sensation you may feel, and any sounds you hear. Allow them to come, and gently let them go. Do not judge or investigate; quietly remind yourself that nothing that comes and goes is you. This will help you to detach from your thoughts and prioritize the nowness of your life.

EXERCISE 2.

Commit to remembering to remain in the now by repeating this phrase whenever you notice yourself obsessively overthinking: "Now is the time to be aware of the present moment. I choose to let go of the past and the future."

NO MATTER HOW MUCH YOUR LIFE CHANGES, ONE THING IS CERTAIN; IT'S ALWAYS NOW

– ECKHART TOLLE

STEP 3

WHAT YOU THINK, YOU BECOME

Now that you are becoming more attuned to your conscious awareness and practicing mindfulness here and now, you are ready for another undisclosed truth to be revealed to you. In this chapter, I want to talk to you about the power of your thoughts; specifically about the power of vibration your thoughts emit. All things in our Universe are constantly in motion, vibrating. Quantum physics tells us that everything vibrates and everything is energy. Even objects that appear to be solid and stationary are rapidly vibrating at an atomic level and resonating at various frequencies. Human beings are no exception. Despite your physical appearance of skin, bones, and organs, you have always been an energetic/vibrational being living in a vibrational universe (Hicks, 2004).

You are cognizant of your physical experience and the external world through your innate ability to interpret vibration. Through your five sensory organs, you're able to translate the vibration around you to that which you can see, hear, smell, touch, and taste. Thanks to the specialized cells and tissues within your sensory organs, they receive and translate raw stimuli into signals which the nervous system then relays to the brain, interpreting them. Additionally, you emit a vibrational signal through your thoughts and emotions. Both thoughts and emotions are cosmic waves filled with potent energy. There is tremendous power when you deliberately choose what you think and how you feel. You may be familiar with the universal law of attraction (the most popular universal law): for whatever you strongly think about, you emit a vibration. That vibration, by universal law, is then required to come to you. For every thought pulsates, every thought emits a signal, and every thought invites an equivalent signal back. Thus, you are a vibrational broadcaster (Hicks, 2004).

Whenever you put your attention and focus upon a thought (whether it be positive or negative), you energize the vibration of the thought within yourself (Hicks, 2004). Can you recall an incident when you thought of something you didn't want to experience or something you didn't want in your life, and yet it somehow entered into the content of your life? Or perhaps there was a time when you strongly desired something that you couldn't stop thinking about, for it to then magically manifest into your physical reality? This is very similar to switching on your radio and intentionally adjusting your receiver to harmonize with the signal of your favorite station. Whether you think of something you do not want or think of something you do want, your focus and attention on that specific thought is what summons it into your physical experience. What you concentrate on and what the Universe gives you is always a faultless vibrational match (Hicks, 2004).

As you become accustomed to referring to yourself as a vibrational being, I must clarify that I am not encouraging you to forcefully control your thoughts. Rather, strive to steer your thoughts. But, even more than that, move towards a "feeling" you wish to experience (Hicks, 2004). When you feel good and happy, you produce joyous thoughts. The same concept applies when you feel angry and sad, you produce thoughts that correlate to those feelings. Your most complicated and perplexing vibrational interpreter is your emotions. They assist you with grasping, here and now, the experiences that you are living out. Emotions can be seen as a guidance system that alerts your conscious awareness of how you feel in your moment-to-moment experience (Hicks, 2004). By being aware of your emotions, you become aware of the kind of vibration you are emitting. How you feel will always be parallel to what you are thinking in your minute-by-minute experience. It will be beneficial for you to embark on being conscious of how you are feeling, what you are thinking, and what is happening in your life experience. For example, if you feel grateful for the abundance of money you have (regardless of how little or large) and think deeply about how you enjoy spending money on vacations; you may see that more money flows to you, allowing you to travel more. On the other hand, if you feel anxious about your vacation and anticipate that something bad will occur during the vacation, you may see that something indeed did go bad just as you predicted. That which you feel and think, you vibrate, emit, and become. By accepting yourself as an energetic/vibrational being, you assume the responsibility of attracting all the things that come into your life (Hicks, 2004). Once you begin seeing the inter-relationship between how you are feeling, what you are thinking, and what is manifesting in your experience, the power of intentionally co-creating your life is realized. I challenge you to choose to be a person who is actively and consciously thinking and guiding their thoughts to ultimately become the master of their minds.

PRACTICES FOR CHAPTER 3

EXERCISE 1.

Practice being mindful of your thoughts and how you feel in every waking moment of your life. Any time an undesirable thought arises, accept the thought without fear. This will help you to bypass the thought without being emotionally conflicted. After accepting it, replace the negative thought with a positive thought; this helps you reprogram your thinking pattern, enabling you to sway your thoughts.

EXERCISE 2.

Focus your attention on what you do have and what you desire. Focusing on whatever it is you may lack or do not want is counterintuitive and invites a vibrational match of scarcity into the content of your life. Practice gratitude for the little things in life, and observe how the Universe gives you more to be joyful about.

THOUGHT IS NOT REALITY, YET IT IS THROUGH THOUGHT THAT OUR REALITIES ARE CREATED

– SYDNEY BANKS

STEP 4

EMOTIONALLY ACCEPT WHATEVER IS HERE-AND-NOW

Before I get into the fourth step, I wish for you to acknowledge how far you have come to ultimately master your heart and mind. You have relearned distinct truths that include you being the conscious awareness that is observing your thoughts, feelings, and interactions with others; how it is your emotional programming, fixations, and ego that creates your actions—which also influences the reaction of other people around you (Keyes, 1975); seeing through the illusion of time; understanding there is only a singular moment in time (which is now); and that whatever you choose to think and feel in your moment-to-moment experience, you offer a vibration that attracts a matching vibration into your physical reality. It is because you have come this far that Chapter Four is here to propel you even further into your journey. This step is one of the most potent ways to protect your inner peace as it steadily grows.

In this chapter, I want to encourage you to establish the routine of emotionally accepting whatever is here and now in your life. I am encouraging you to do so because, in this life, you only have control over one thing: yourself. There are still numerous individuals who are controlled by their emotional programming and ego. They cannot perceive life clearly, and every time the outside world does not abide by the way they desire and expect it to be, they automatically trigger an unpleasant emotion as their response. You can either unconsciously get caught up emotionally in others' actions or consciously choose to accept whatever is occurring. There is a deep level of serenity in emotionally accepting whatever is here and now in your life. You regain the power to choose how you respond and feel in any given situation. An illustration: let's say you are jogging through your neighborhood and you suddenly drop your new phone you bought last week. As you pick it up, your entire front screen is shattered, and it won’t turn back on. To make matters worse, you haven't bought insurance for it because you have never broken any of your previous phones. As a result, you automatically respond with a triggering emotion of disappointment, worry, anger, sadness, regret, and frustration. These emotions will not and cannot reverse the nowness of your life. All they do is take away from your inner peace and energy to then shift you into a more oppressed mind state. But, when you emotionally accept whatever is here and now, you can then choose how you feel and your next course of action. Yes, you may feel frustrated initially, but like all other emotions, it will come and go. There is either a solution or not to fix your new phone. You can either do something about it at that moment or you cannot. If you can do something about it now, great; take the necessary steps! If there is no immediate solution that you can try here and now, why make yourself feel restless and antsy (Keyes, 1975)? Worrying or being frustrated only takes away from your inner peace and energy. The quicker you recognize that uncomfortable emotions are unnecessary, the quicker you can begin to safeguard your happiness.

As you accept what is the nowness of your life, you are allowing life to be just as it is without trying to distort it. Remember, your wants, requirements, and expectations of the world and all those residing within it, are what make you feel upset when those expectations are not met (Keyes, 1975). Now, I am not telling you to accept being in a situation where someone may be mistreating or undervaluing you. Acceptance simply means that you are willing to tolerate difficult or unpleasant situations without changing them or protesting them so that you are not emotionally conflicted. Therefore, when you emotionally accept where that person is coming from, you can then choose the best course of action for you and your well-being. You can aspire to eliminate unnecessary worrying and any other unpleasant emotions, in order to maintain your center of peace within your heart and mind. Emotionally accepting whatever your life has to offer you allows you to do just that! You will begin to see for yourself how, with each passing minute, you continue to be happy. You are no longer on a roller coaster of emotions and thoughts that randomly happen to you. The power to choose what you feel and what you think all resides within you, all you have to do is accept the nowness of your life.

PRACTICES FOR CHAPTER 4

EXERCISE 1.

Practice emotionally accepting whatever is here and now. Be patient with yourself and others as you practice this technique. This exercise will help you overcome any obstacle that life may place before you and keep you feeling joyful.

EXERCISE 2.

Before starting each day, affirm with this Reiki affirmation: "Just for today, I will not worry. Just for today, I will not be angry. Just for today, I will be thankful for all my blessings. Just for today, I will be compassionate and understanding. Just for today, I will be at peace."

KEEP IN MIND: THE MORE WE VALUE THINGS OUTSIDE OUR CONTROL, THE LESS CONTROL WE HAVE.

– EPICTETUS

STEP 5
TRUST

In this chapter, I will talk to you about learning to trust your conscious awareness (higher self) and God (Source, the Universe, etc.). While this is not a religious text, through my own life experience and experiences of others, I have learned that God is very much existent, whether we wish to believe it or not. As stated in Chapter One, who we undeniably are is sheer conscious awareness. Our conscious awareness comes directly from this cosmic intelligence which I will title as God—the intelligence that created all things: animals, plants, water, galaxies, stars, planets, the moon—the list goes on. To put this into perspective, let's take your body as an example. You have no control of whether or not your heart beats, the amount of saliva your mouth produces, your ability to heal from a cut, and so forth. The human body has so many autonomous features to keep itself healthy and running that we are unaware of most of the things it does until we are either injured or become ill. But, it does not stop at us humans; let's take mother Gaia (Earth) as another example. Due to the Earth's orbital velocity working against the sun's gravitational pull, Earth is out of harm's way from falling towards the sun. It is at a perfect distance from the sun, where we are neither frozen to death nor set ablaze. Trees are planted and programmed to help us breathe by taking in the carbon dioxide we breathe out to then send out oxygen, through photosynthesis, for humans to survive. Even animals have a built-in mechanism that allows them to survive and adapt on Earth.

No human being possesses the absolute intelligence and extraordinary power to do all these things except for God. As you are learning from the previous steps and begin to tune into your higher self, you will realize that it has always been present, leading you to your heart's deepest desires. Tuning into your higher self, you'll notice that you get bodily sensations that are meant to guide you to make decisions that are in your best interest. A quick example is when you feel your lower stomach tightening when you suspect something is wrong or someone is being deceitful. There is a reason as to why we have these sensations; they are meant to alert and guide us to safety. By continually listening and trusting your conscious awareness, you connect with your higher self, intuitively becoming the person you've been destined to be. But, for you to see your dreams come to fruition and silence your inner critic, it is imperative that you have faith. While it is difficult to walk not by sight, but by faith, you can choose to let go of constantly worrying and feeling anxious about what is next to come. Have faith that your higher self knows what is best for you. Have faith that you can create the life you long desire. Have faith that whoever created mankind wants to see all of us happy and loving.

Finally, surrender to the nowness of your life and trust that whatever is happening in your experience is for your highest good. This level of trust is something that needs to be built over time, similarly with any kind of relationship. For when you develop this trust in yourself and God, you free your rational mind from trying to perfectly plan out your life in fine detail. And as you may already know, nothing in life goes exactly as planned. We only create anxiety and fear for ourselves, which exhausts our energy. Have faith that your conscious awareness is efficiently directing you through life, conclusively bringing you closer to your heart's deepest desires. It may also be worth pointing out that you have overcome all your past worries that made you feel anxious and fearful; still, you stand, and for some, it may have happened in a way you couldn't even imagine. As I expressed in the last chapter, all that you can control is yourself. Planning in great detail and trying to figure out how everything will fall into place keeps you from enjoying the here and now. You did not make it this far to only come this far. You are meant to continuously evolve and adapt; it is only human nature.

To conclude this chapter, I wish to use an example to tie this all together. Whether someone is religious or not, in a dire life or death situation, most people will say, "God help me!" Or if they need help in a tough situation they say, "God, if you help me with this, I'll never do that again." When we desperately need a miracle, we call on God. Your conscious awareness, together with God, knows no bounds and makes the impossible very much possible. So instead of burdening yourself with the hows and whens, trust that life, your higher self, and God will give you everything you need when you need it. I have come to understand that the creator of all things simply wants to have a relationship with its creation. You do not have to go through your life's journey alone.

PRACTICES FOR STEP 5

EXERCISE 1.

Permit yourself to live your life without outside influence. The more authentic YOU can be, the more you will learn about yourself. This will help you establish how you really feel and what you really want, rather than doing what others think you should be doing.

EXERCISE 2.

Write down all the things you like about yourself including your strengths. This helps you to see just how impactful you are and the many unique qualities you possess.

EXERCISE 3.

Make time to be alone with yourself. By getting used to being on your own, you will learn to become more comfortable with yourself, your thoughts, and your emotions. All this will help you to build up a trusting relationship with yourself.

EXERCISE 4.

Practice reading your body language; checking in with yourself allows you to connect more deeply with your heart and mind.

The more you know yourself, the more you can predict what you'll do. The more you learn to trust yourself, the more faith you'll have in your actions.

EXERCISE 5.

Give yourself time to grow your relationship with yourself and God. You can nurture these relationships by being patient, positively reinforcing good behaviors, and keeping an open mind.

EXERCISE 6.

Practice surrendering your goals, ambitions, and dreams to the Universe and trust that what you need will be given to you in divine timing. Your success is inevitable; learn to enjoy the journey more than the final results of the journey. Journey>Destination.

BE STILL AND KNOW
I AM GOD

STEP 6
BREATHING

In this chapter, I want to talk to you about the importance of your breath, its impact on your rational mind, and how you feel. By closing your eyes and taking in slow, deep breaths, not only can you overcome stress, but you can also manage anxiety and anger. This method is known as vagal breathing, which gets its name from the vagus nerve, the most complex and extensive distributor of the 12 cranial nerves that link the brain to the rest of the body (Chopra, 2020). It connects the brain with the lungs, abdomen, and heart. These three areas are particularly sensitive to stress. The vagus nerve is also known as a sensory nerve that relays bodily impulses to the brain; this includes reactions accompanied by stress. Therefore, whenever you find yourself in a stressful scenario, your heart rate soars, your breath is irregular, and you feel a tightening in your lower stomach. To activate a relaxation response, all you have to do is stimulate the vagus nerve by taking slow, deep, and relaxed breaths (Chopra, 2020). How simplistic and readily accessible this is for anyone to use in any situation. While knowledge is power, it is the implementation of knowledge that grants you true power. You may have never heard of vagal breathing up to this point. However, it is now up to you to be conscious of your breath when you feel stressed, worried, and angry so you can activate a relaxation response. In doing so, you reap the benefits of being in a more relaxed and joyous state; which supports your conscious awareness in its ability to maneuver and guide you through life more efficiently. You then can perceive life and others from a calmer and higher vantage point, allowing you to come up with solutions quicker and easier.

For example, let's say you are in the grocery store and you overhear two people bickering over the last rolls of toilet paper. As you get closer to the aisle they're in, you see that they are both on edge and stressed. One is yelling, with their adversary reacting with more yelling. All the while, there is another roll of toilet paper on the top shelf. It is not as though you have enhanced visual prowess; they merely cannot perceive the situation for what it truly is and prefer to make it a contest of who's "right" and who's "wrong." People tend to be mirrors that reflect whatever energetic state you are in. If you are stressed and hostile, those around you will appear stressed and hostile. Vice versa, if you're happy and calm, those around you will appear happy and calm. This holds to be true even in the example. As the Greek Stoic philosopher, Epictetus, once said, “Any person capable of angering you becomes your master.”

Ergo, in the process of learning how to master your heart and mind, knowing how you can calm yourself here and now is absolutely essential. You cannot maneuver through life with ease and joy if you are constantly in fight-or-flight mode. Vagal breathing and any other yogic breathing is the key to re-centering yourself, bringing you back inwardly to your conscious awareness.

Something that I have come to learn and integrate into my life is a mantra that dials in on re-centering and recalibrating my thoughts and vibration. It has been exceedingly useful and I wish to share it with you. However, this mantra is not mine, and I do not take credit for it. The mantra came from the late Ken Keyes Jr.; may he continue to rest in peace. It goes, "All Ways Us Living Love." Chanting mantras is an ancient practice that aids in calming your heart and mind. Chanting this and other mantras, your mind lovingly releases the positive energy that diminishes negative thoughts, feelings, and stress. While you are conscious of your breathing, repeat the words, "All Ways Us Living Love," over and over. It can be sung, spoken aloud, whispered, or repeated within your mind. Repeat and meditate on it for five to 10 minutes, and notice how you feel afterward. You may feel a deep sense of stillness and connection to everything around you. What I love about this mantra and vagal breathing is that you can do both at any given moment. Use these two techniques to relieve your mind and heart from unpleasant thoughts and emotions, to then swiftly usher in a wave of relaxation and inner peace.

PRACTICES FOR CHAPTER 6

EXERCISE 1.

Practice vagal breathing. **1).** Comfortably sit where you won't be distracted and gently close your eyes. Allow your lower belly to expand on the inhale and let it sink back towards your spine on the exhale. **2).** Gently inhale through your nose for a count of four. While inhaling, lightly press your tongue on the roof of your mouth. **3).** Hold your breath for a count of three. **4).** Slowly exhale through your mouth for a count of four, then pause for a moment before inhaling again. Repeat this process for five to 10 minutes (you can steadily increase the time) each day, and you will see that you're much calmer, more focused, happier, healthier, and lighter.

EXERCISE 2.

Recite Ken Keyes Jr.'s mantra. While doing your vagal breathing, repeat the mantra " All Ways Us Living Love." Exaggerate and emphasize each word. You can say this mantra aloud or in your mind. Consistent repetition will help you calm your mind, keep you feeling joyful, and increase your ability to concentrate. Ensure you are not operating any vehicle when you're first practicing this mantra.

THE BREATH IS THE
KING OF THE MIND

– B.K.S IYENGAR

STEP 7
LOVE UNCONDITIONALLY

In this final chapter, I want to talk to you about the most powerful and therapeutic method known to mankind used to illuminate all the traumatic life experiences you have endured thus far in order to heal your inner child. Unfortunately, the majority of us have been misinformed; we were never taught what real, unconditional love looks like. Many of us are mistaken when we take that which is conditional love as unconditional love. The programming of the Western world has been to manipulate and force situations to get whatever it desires; this includes both receiving and giving love. However, something so pure cannot be manipulated or forced upon someone. Rather, love is soft, tranquil, and flows smoothly like a river. Think of conditional love as a transaction where people exchange certain demands for their love. We have been taught that we have to be deemed worthy for us to receive love, having to feel the urgency to continually prove ourselves in the hope we can be loved.

Likewise, we tell ourselves that others have to be deserving to receive our love as if we have a daily limit. For example, you may have been in a love situation where your partner said something like, "If you love me, you will do this for me." When your emotional programming, alongside its fixations, dominates your consciousness, you tend to leverage love to fulfill your needs and/or wants. Uncon-ditional love is not something you fight for, use as a bargaining chip, or use to manipulate others. Unconditional love is just love. It is merely accepting everyone and everything around you completely and unconditionally.

You love someone simply because they exist and are a part of the nowness of your life. Just being born into this world, you are loved. Even on your worst days, despite your worst mistakes, you have, at all times, been lovable. A notable example to help put this into greater perspective is to think about a child who has behavioral problems such as lying and being disobedient. Although they are not behaving the way someone expects or demands them to, does it mean they are no longer lovable? Of course not! This applies to everyone, even adults who still behave in a manner that indicates they have yet to heal their wounded inner child or from their past traumas.

There are countless individuals of all ages, fiercely holding onto their pain, not understanding that their pain is vigorously growing with each passing day. Hence, the reason why so many of us try to escape our realities through sex, drugs, alcohol, and entertainment. When wanting to reflect on a painful experience, that in itself can already be too agonizing. So rather than trying to reflect, heal, and release, we continue to distract ourselves from our painful experiences and act like we are okay when internally, we are suffering continuous misery.

As you remember from the very first chapter, we all developed our emotional programming in our youth from being severely dominated, pushed around, and always told what to do, feel, and be. At some point in your life, you have experienced something traumatic that forced you to shift the way you think and feel, as well as the things you say and do. There may be things you have experienced that you have never spoken to anyone about. There may have been a time when someone you trusted ended up betraying and hurting you. There may be a situation you recall where someone took advantage of you. Any incident that has caused you physical, emotional, sexual, social, spiritual, mental, or psychological harm, tampers with how you love yourself and others around you. As mere children, we do not fully grasp why or how we endured such suffering. Many of us grow up trying to forget or grow out of our past traumatic experiences in the hope of being better in the future. While this is admirable, the inner child is still suffering, which is reflected in our actions, thoughts, words, and feelings. Repression is one of the most harmful and unconscious things you can do to yourself. When you repress these types of experiences and the emotions that came with them, your body stores and holds all the negative energy within itself. Negative emotions can be stored away and felt physically in the following areas (but not limited to): lower back pain, heart and chest pain, trouble breathing, neck and shoulder tension, and hip pain. Withholding these energies within your body is no longer serving you or your higher self. It is time to release these negative emotions and make room for joyful energy to come in. You may have heard the saying, "The only way out is through." To truly master your heart and mind, you must be willing to face your darkest experiences head-on and come out victorious.

Furthermore, you must understand that whatever traumatic experience you went through, it was never your fault. You mustn't blame yourself for someone else's actions, nor should you feel ashamed. Learn to forgive those who have caused you pain, turmoil, and suffering, for your own sake. When you carry the burden of not forgiving the wrong someone has done, you limit your happiness and inner peace. Any time something reminds you of that specific incident, your emotional programming will be triggered, leaving you anxious, fearful, and incapable of perceiving life for what it truly is. The ego then enforces you to identify with the triggering emotion and see everyone as a threat to you, limiting your ability to love yourself and others. I am not asking you to forgive those who wronged you because they deserve a second chance. Rather, I am asking you to forgive because it is your absolute birthright to be loving and joyful. Forgiveness not only brings a piece of serenity that supports you to continue onwards with life, but it also provokes the emotions of understanding, empathy, and compassion for the one(s) who hurt you. Forgiving someone doesn't mean forgetting or excusing the harm done to you. As you learned in Chapter 4 (emotionally accept whatever is here-and-now), you too will need to practice emotionally accepting your past.

Accepting your past will be a work in progress rather than a one-day fix. You will need to practice accepting your darkness. Every dark experience has played its part in molding you into who you are today. You can either allow it to define who you are or embrace the pain, enabling it to be your power to become something greater. It is for you and only you, that you should accept all things in your deceased past. Bringing the pain of yesterday into each new day hinders your ability to create the life you deserve. You are entitled to be free from the emotional pain of your past.

Whatever traumatic experience you have endured, you are and always will be a pillar of light. Your past does not define who you are or where you are going. Now is the time to muster up the courage to be willing to reflect back on all your traumatic life experiences and allow yourself to feel and sit with the emotions that are attached to them. Do not fight or shy away from them. Welcome them and simply sit with them, allowing yourself to stretch your range and depth of emotions. Visualize each experience in your mind, feel the emotions that each memory stimulates, and know that what you are feeling is not who you are. This can be extremely difficult at first, but persevere and proceed to replay the same memories over and over and over again. Each time, remind yourself that you are no longer in that situation and that you are safe. Use this technique to seize back your power from those who caused you suffering. Continue this practice until you reach the point where you do not feel triggered emotionally, spiritually, or mentally. Luckily, there is no due date for when you should be fully healed. Thus, avoid placing expectations on the speed at which you think you should be healed. For healing is an everyday process that aids you in remembering who you are. Recognize that your healing process is unique and meant solely for you. Claim it with excitement and allow yourself to take all the time you need! Stay away from comparing yourself to others and harshly criticizing your past. All you have is here and now; you have the power to use every negative experience and all its energy to transmute it into the strength needed for you to actualize your wildest dreams.

When you begin to love everything about yourself, including your flaws and past, your world becomes a happier world to live in. Love is infinite and everlasting; there is immense power in loving yourself. Allow love to be your strength to overcome any and every dark experience. Let go of your past with grace and acknowledge that you are free to go after your heart's deepest desires. Once you arrive at a place in time where you can emotionally accept your past and love yourself unconditionally, you will have successfully healed your inner child. You become the person that comforts and loves the wounded child within yourself instead of hoping and waiting for someone else to. This sort of alchemy that occurs within you will grant you great serenity in who you are and where you are going. It awards you the choice to move forward with love to create a fulfilling and blissful life. With every thought, intention, and action from this point onwards, I challenge you to do these things with love. In doing so, you will begin to see how beautifully the Universe and those around you love you back.

As we begin to wrap up this book, I want you to always remember that you are loved and that you are more than capable of realizing your heart's deepest desires into your physical reality. Please, be patient with yourself throughout all the steps and enjoy the journey of becoming the best version of yourself. Gaining the strength of controlling your heart and mind is one of the greatest accomplishments for any human being. I understand that if you implement the information that I have shared, you will surely have full mastery of your heart and mind. As you continue to learn and practice, you will gradually expand and evolve minute-by-minute. On the other side of discomfort and pain lies bliss and growth. Even so, the journey towards within is no simple task. If you feel though this is something you need help executing, I would be honored to assist you step-by-step.

From my experience as an emotional intelligence practitioner and spiritual life coach, I have accumulated a wealth of knowledge that has allowed me to heal and love more intensely despite living in this corrupted world. I've always had an intense longing to help and save others. So much so, I lost myself countless times for the sake of helping others. Through losing my sense of purpose, I quickly learned that I can't help and save everyone. But more importantly, I can't help others if I don't know how to help myself. It wasn't until recently, I conceived the idea of creating a step-by-step process of how I healed and mastered myself. While everyone's life lessons are different, one lesson that remains constant within everyone's path is learning how to heal and move forward with love. Rather than continuing to try to help and save everyone blindly (hurting myself in the process), I've been called to create a book and coaching program that would reveal a pathway that guides everyone back to their inner light so they can save themselves. As Martin Luther King Jr. stated, "Darkness cannot drive out darkness; only light can do that. Hate cannot drive out hate; only love can do that." If you're determined to reflect, heal, release, and love, this next paragraph is devoted to you.

I have developed a 1-on-1 coaching program that will break down each step (in greater detail) with several healing techniques to support you in reprogramming your emotional programming, aligning with your conscious awareness, silencing your ego and inner critic, facing and healing past trauma, protecting your inner peace, and loving yourself unconditionally. For once you have full control of yourself, there is nothing you cannot do. No person can destroy you, no experience can derail you, and no obstacle can stop you. You will have claimed your rightful place as the co-creator of your world, living a life filled with peace, love, and joy. I want to thank you from the deepest depths of my heart for supporting this book. I am eager to see the results you attain from executing the exercises, and if you decide to move forward with my coaching program, I can't wait to add more value there. Please take a moment to follow me on Instagram @injoshua_wetrust_.

PRACTICES FOR CHAPTER 7

EXERCISE 1.

Emotionally accept and forgive your past alongside all your traumatic experiences by visualizing each experience and intentionally re-triggering yourself. Allow yourself to sit with and feel all the emotions that arise when remembering each experience. The point of this practice is to allow all that pain and the unpleasant emotions to resurface so that you can guide them out of your nervous system. Cry and yell if you need to, but if you truly want to conquer yourself, you will need to face your darkness. Continue this method until you reach the point where you no longer feel those triggering emotions. Towards the end of each session, remind yourself that you are safe and no longer in those situations. Lastly, take your time and ease into this process. Using this practice, deep emotional pain will resurface, so I suggest taking small steps in healing your inner child. The first step to healing is to look inwardly and allow the process of releasing to begin.

EXERCISE 2.

Practice accepting everyone completely and unconditionally. Despite the craziest, most absurd actions or words someone does or says, accept them just as they are. This will help you from judging yourself and others as you continue to practice loving unconditionally.

EXERCISE 3.

Write down the things you love about yourself and the things you dislike about yourself. The objective here is to feel empowered when you read your strengths along with your flaws/weaknesses. Learn to accept and embrace your flaws and weaknesses, for they too, are what make you…you.

EXERCISE 4.

Remove toxic people around you who make you feel guilty for loving yourself. Begin to surround yourself with people who continually uplift you and love you through all your madness. This will help you love yourself more effectively.

EXERCISE 5.

Continually face your inner obstacles and resistance with love. This means facing your weaknesses and flaws with compassion and understanding. Instead of judging and criticizing yourself, choose to love yourself completely, equipping yourself with the strength to not only face these things, but to improve them.

EXERCISE 6.

Accept where you are right now. Remind yourself that you are not the person you once were, and choose to move forward with love in your heart. You can use the nowness of your life to either burden yourself with the wounds of painful memories of your past or use it to intentionally create the life you have always dreamt about. Acceptance allows you to finally be free and chase your wildest dreams.

EXERCISE 7.

Practice giving the kind of love you aspire to receive. If you want someone to be gentle, loving, romantic, sweet, or catering, be all of these things for yourself first. You cannot expect someone to love you properly if you do not love yourself. This will help you to be mindful of how loving you are in your moment-to-moment experience.

RESOURCES

Chopra, Deepak. (2020). *Total meditation*. Harmony Books.

Hicks, Esther, & Hicks, Jerry. (2004). *Ask and It Is Given: Learning to Manifest Your Desires. Hay House.*

Keyes, Ken. *Handbook to Higher Consciousness*. Living Love Center, 1974.

Tolle, Eckhart. (2003). *Stillness Speaks*. New World Library.

NOTES

NOTES

NOTES

NOTES

NOTES

NOTES

NOTES

NOTES

NOTES

Made in the USA
Columbia, SC
15 March 2024

32760718R00043